TEACHER CREATURES

TONY LEE AND MARC ELLERBY

LONDON·SYDNEY

YOU'RE NEW, RIGHT?

I'M BETH RAINEY – BUT EVERYONE CALLS ME **BRAINY**.

ER – HI, BRAINY.

THAT WAS **VIKKI**. SHE THINKS SHE RUNS THE SCHOOL.

HER MUM'S A SCHOOL GOVERNOR – SO **SHE** NEVER GETS INTO TROUBLE.

NOT **ALL** OF US ARE LIKE HER THOUGH.

YOU'VE TOLD YOUR PARENTS ABOUT TONIGHT'S **PARENT-TEACHER MEETING**?

IT'S **COMPULSORY** FOR THEM TO ATTEND!

NO ATTENDANCE EQUALS **DEMERITS**.

REALLY? WE WEREN'T TOLD THIS.

THAT'S NOT FAIR!

THE SCHOOL OFFICE.

SHERIDAN ACADEMY

EXCUSE ME - IS THE **HEADTEACHER** HERE?

WE NEED TO SPEAK TO HER.

IT'S ABOUT TONIGHT'S MEETING.

I DO HOPE THAT YOUR PARENTS ARE COMING.

IT WOULD BE **TERRIBLE** FOR YOU IF THEY CAN'T COME.

BUT IT'S OUR FIRST DAY. WE WEREN'T TOLD.

WE'LL NEED TO CALL THEM.

THEN I SUGGEST YOU DO THAT.

THERE WILL BE **NO** EXCEPTIONS TONIGHT.

← THE HEADTEACHER

≥GULP≤

8

THE STAFFROOM.

STAFF ONLY

KNOCK! KNOCK!

HELLO? ANYONE HERE?

ARGH!

JUST SOME **COATS.** SORRY.

CAN YOU HEAR THAT? THERE'S TALKING IN THE NEXT ROOM.

WE SHOULDN'T BE HERE. STAFFROOMS ARE SACRED **TEACHER** GROUND. NO STUDENTS WELCOME!

WE SHOULD HAVE EVERY PARENT OF EVERY STUDENT THERE TONIGHT!

THEY WERE TALKING ABOUT **TONIGHT.** SOMETHING ABOUT THE PARENTS?

IT'S WHY THEY'RE MAKING SURE **EVERY PARENT** TURNS UP TONIGHT.

THEY'RE GOING TO TAKE OVER ALL OF THEIR BODIES! IT'S AN **INVASION!**

THE ONLY HOPE WE HAVE IS **THIS.**

WHAT IS IT?

I SAW ONE OF THE 'TEACHERS' MIXING SOME **LIQUIDS** IN THE CHEMISTRY LAB.

WHEN SHE SPILLED THE MIXTURE IT TOUCHED HER --

AND SHE **EXPLODED.** POP!

ONCE I WORK OUT HOW TO **COPY** IT - WE CAN STOP THEM ALL!

STUDENTS! IN HONOUR OF TONIGHT'S PARENT TEACHER MEETINGS, WE'RE GIVING YOU THE AFTERNOON OFF!

SO GO HOME - AND WE'LL SEE YOU ALL TONIGHT!

YAY!

IN THE CHEMISTRY LAB.

QUICK, BEFORE SOMEONE COMES!

I THINK I'VE GOT IT!

HOW WILL WE KNOW IF IT **WORKS?**

WE WON'T.

GREAT. SO WHAT'S NEXT?

WHAT'S NEXT IS **YOU** ALL SPEND SOME TIME WITH THE HEADTEACHER --

-- AND YOU CAN TELL HER WHY YOU'RE SNEAKING AROUND THE LAB.

IF WE CAN GET THE CHEMICAL MIXTURE INTO THE **WATER SUPPLY** AND SET THE SPRINKLERS OFF --

IT WILL RAIN ON THE ALIENS!

THERE'S GOT TO BE ACCESS TO THE SPRINKLER-PIPE WATER - YOU CAN PUT IT IN THERE.

WE CAN? WHAT ABOUT YOU?

HEY! STOP!

I'M GOING TO CAUSE A **MASSIVE** DISTRACTION!

HELLO, MRS ROGERS. I JUST WANT YOU TO KNOW --

-- THAT I ALWAYS HATED MATHS.

SPLAT!

WE'RE UNDER ATTACK! LEAVE THE SKIN SUIT!

THANK YOU --

COULDN'T LET THEM TURN YOU INTO A **HUMAN ONESIE,** COULD WE?

WAIT - YOU'RE EVIL VIKKI, THE BULLY --

IS THAT WHAT PEOPLE CALL ME? WELL, I'M **TRYING** TO MANAGE MY ANGER.

NOW I'M **TRYING TO SAVE WORLD.**

WHAT ARE THEY DOING?

GIVING YOU TIME! CAN YOU HIT A SPRINKLER FROM HERE?

I CAN TRY.

AND WHERE IS MR PHILIPS?

OH, YOU KNOW. HE'S ALL OVER THE PLACE.

MY NAME IS NASIR. THIS IS MY TWIN BROTHER, ASIF. TODAY IS OUR **FIRST DAY** AT THIS SCHOOL.

THE **STUDENTS** CAN BE TOUGH TO TALK TO, BUT THEY WARM UP FAST.

THE **CARETAKER** IS REALY HELPFUL.

BUT THE **TEACHERS** --

TWANG!

PINK!

PWHHHHISSSSSSSH!

-- THE TEACHERS ARE A BIT WET!

WAIT - IS THAT SULPHUR? OH, NO!

THE **EFFECTS** WERE IMPRESSIVE.

I PREFERRED THE **MUSICAL NUMBER** THE TEACHERS DID LAST YEAR.

YES — IT ALL WORKED PERFECTLY. THEY DIDN'T SUSPECT US AT ALL.

WE EVEN FOUND SOME **HUMANS** TO ASSIST US.

THE **THERMATON THREAT** IS NEUTRALISED — ALL OF THEM ARE **DEAD.**

THE EARTH DEFENCE FORCE IS DISTRACTED BY THE EVENTS OF THE DAY.

IT IS A **PERFECT** TIME TO **START** THE INVASION OF EARTH.

IT REALLY WAS A **FUN** FIRST DAY.

SO, ARE YOU GOING TO GO ON THAT **DATE** WITH BRAINY?

YOU THINK I SHOULD?

I MIGHT DO — AFTER WE **BECOME LORDS OF THE EARTH!**

THE END...

Franklin Watts
First published in Great Britain in 2018 by The Watts Publishing Group

Text copyright © Tony Lee 2018
Illustration copyright © Marc Ellerby 2018

Illustrator: Marc Ellerby
Design Manager: Peter Scoulding
Cover Designer: Cathryn Gilbert
Production Manager: Robert Dale
Series Consultant: Paul Register
Executive Editor: Adrian Cole

HB ISBN 978 1 4451 5717 7
PB ISBN 978 1 4451 5718 4
Library ebook ISBN 978 1 4451 5719 1

Printed in China

Franklin Watts
An imprint of
Hachette Children's Group
Part of The Watts Publishing Group
Carmelite House
50 Victoria Embankment
London EC4Y 0DZ

An Hachette UK Company
www.hachette.co.uk

www.franklinwatts.co.uk

TEACHER
CREATURES